Chemistry Lab Mysteries, Fun Laboratory Tools! Chemistry for Kids

Children's Analytic Chemistry Books

Doing experiments is a fun activity. When doing laboratory activities, there are many tools to be used. Read on to learn about some of these tools. Learn and have fun!

Beakers

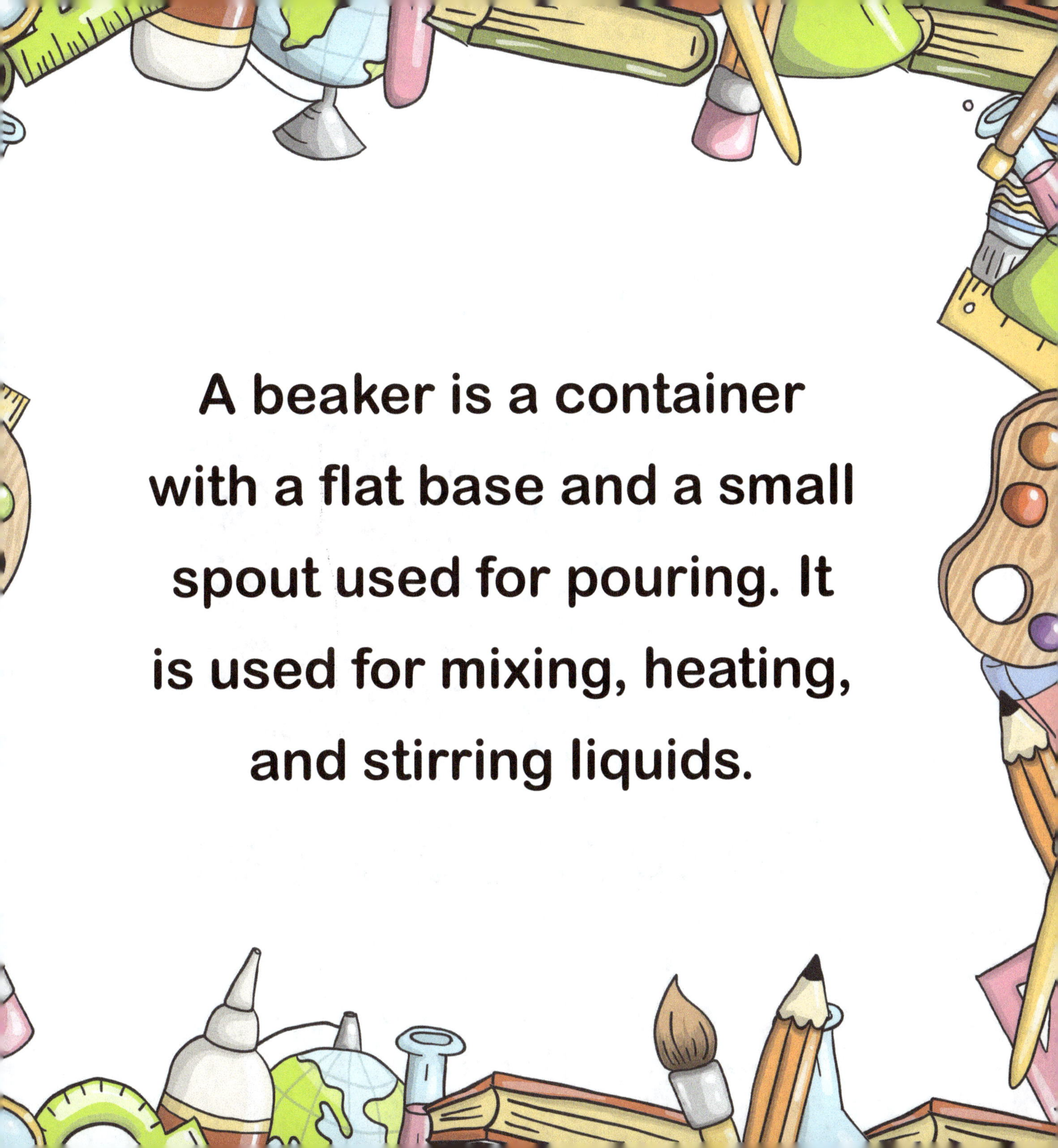

A beaker is a container with a flat base and a small spout used for pouring. It is used for mixing, heating, and stirring liquids.

Reagent Bottles

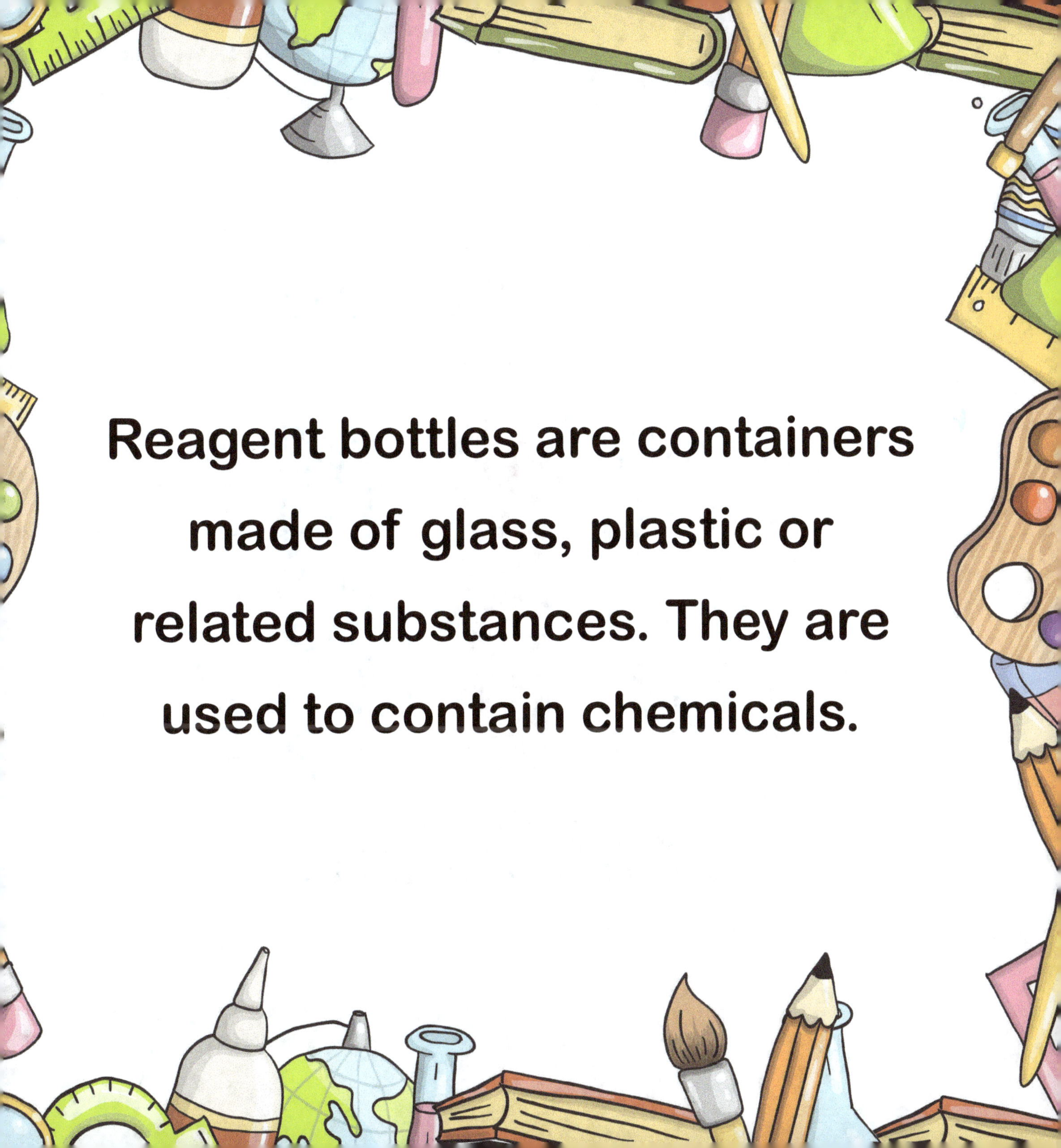

Reagent bottles are containers made of glass, plastic or related substances. They are used to contain chemicals.

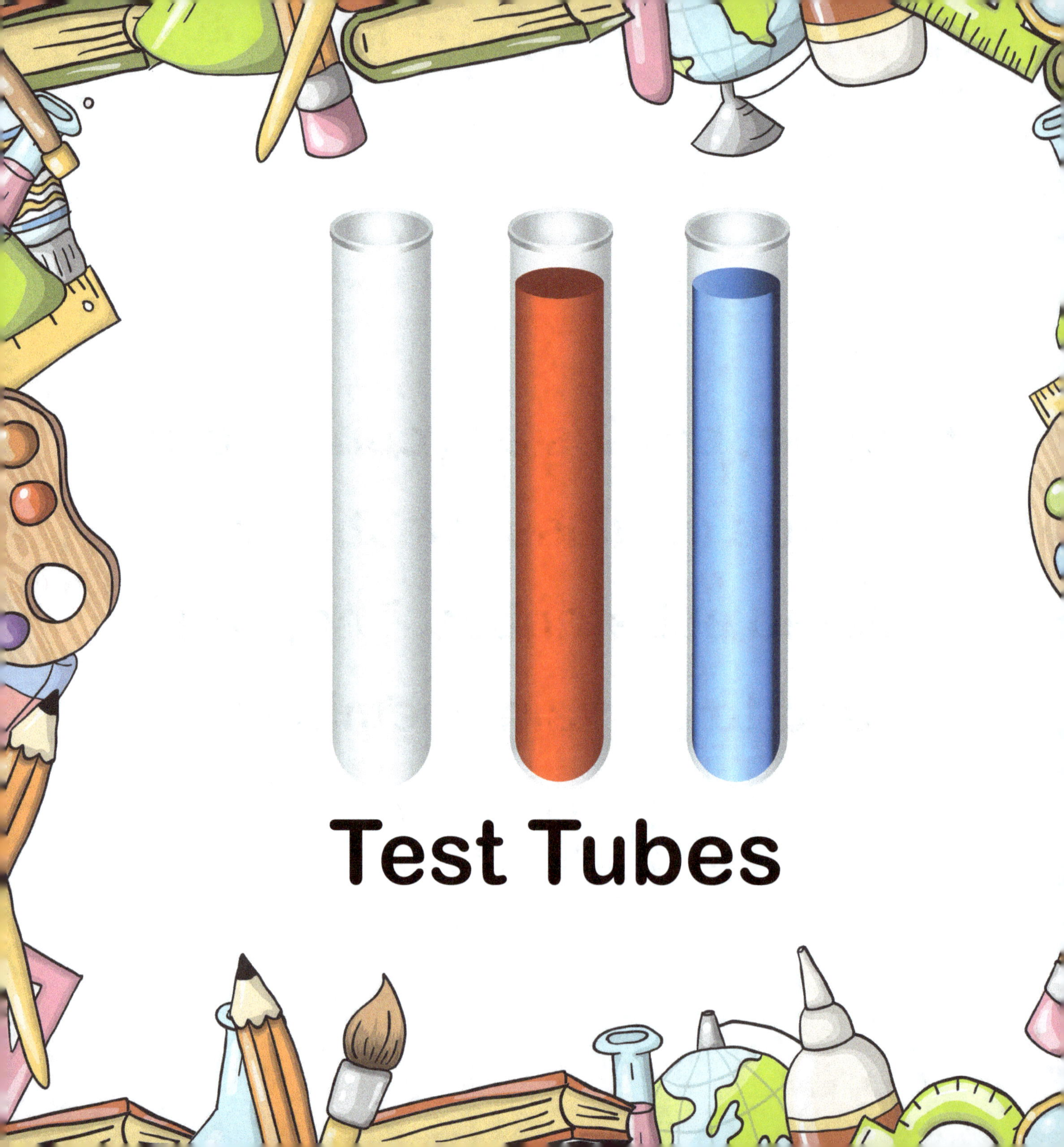
Test Tubes

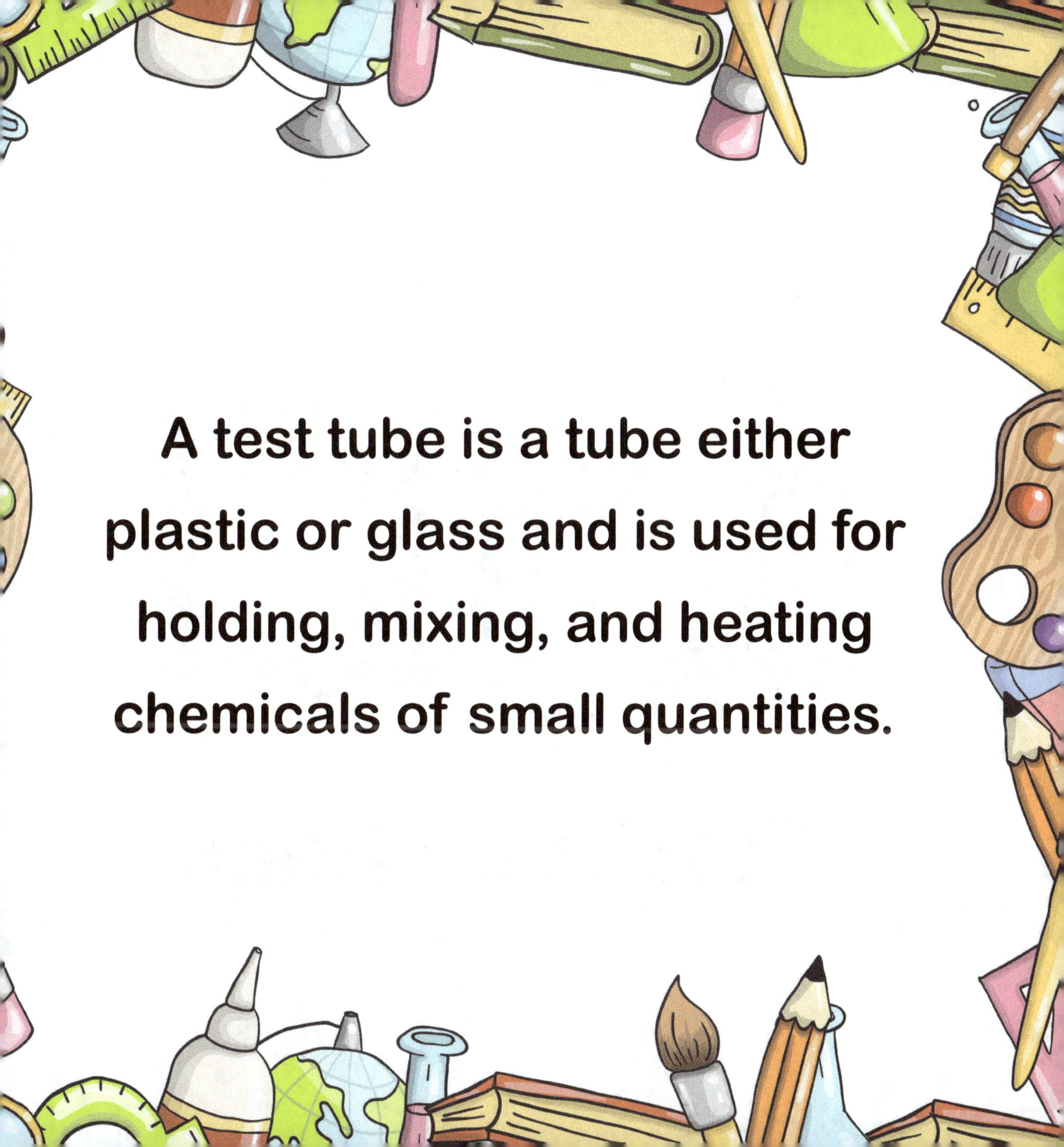

A test tube is a tube either plastic or glass and is used for holding, mixing, and heating chemicals of small quantities.

Test Tube Rack

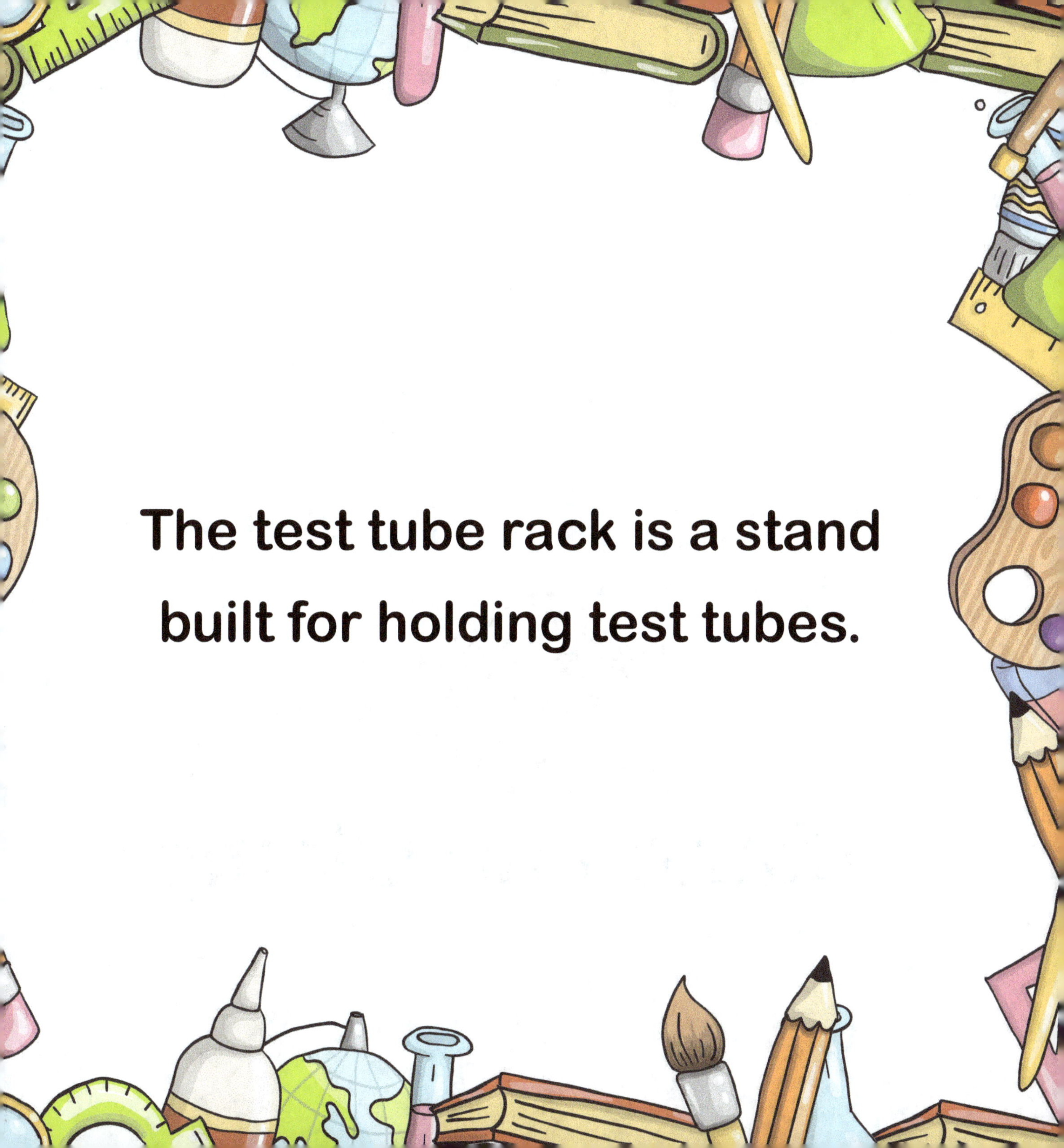

The test tube rack is a stand built for holding test tubes.

Stand and Clamp

This is used to specifically hold and secure a flask on a stand so it would be more convenient for an experiment.

Microscope

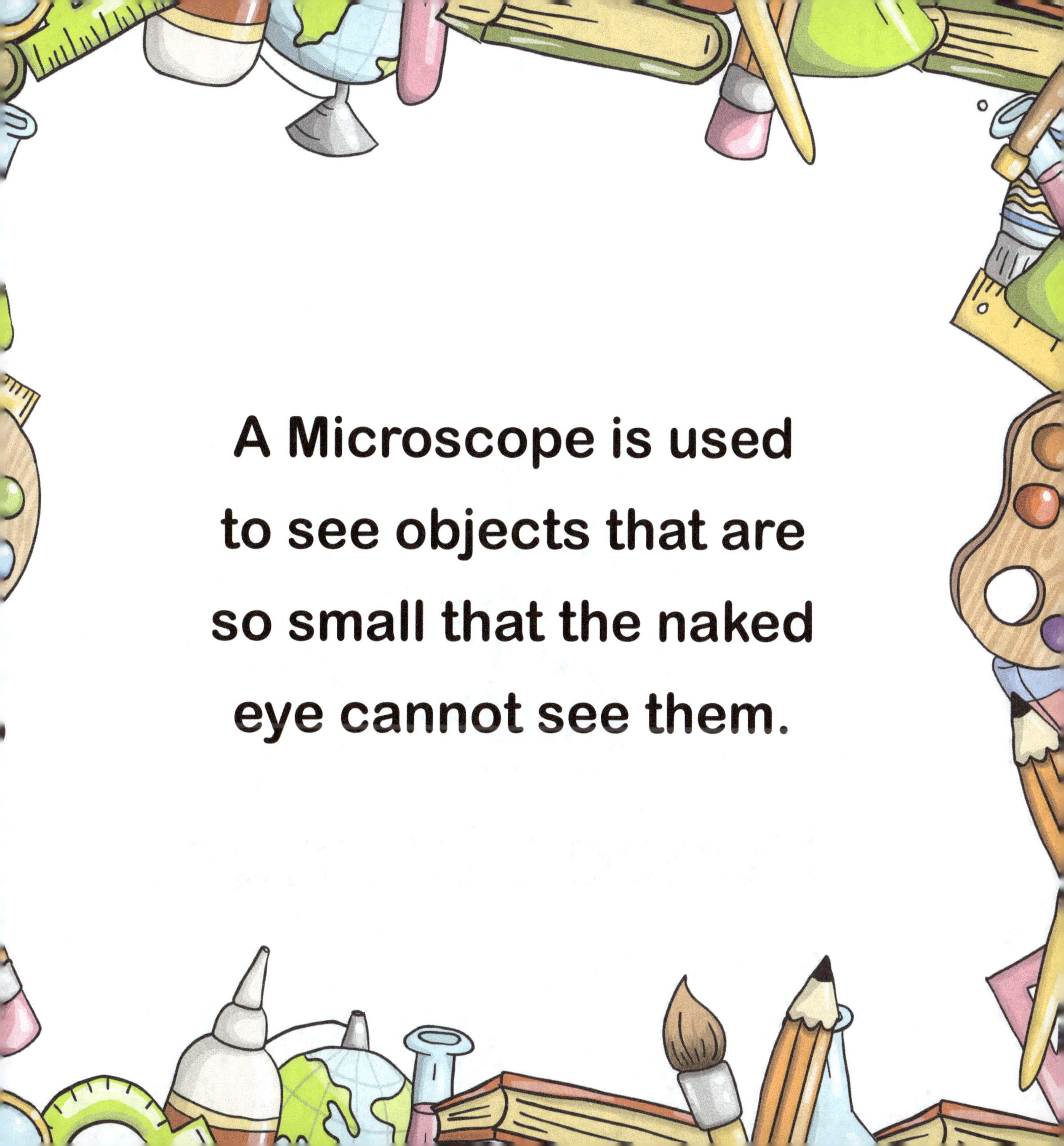

A Microscope is used
to see objects that are
so small that the naked
eye cannot see them.

Bunsen Burner

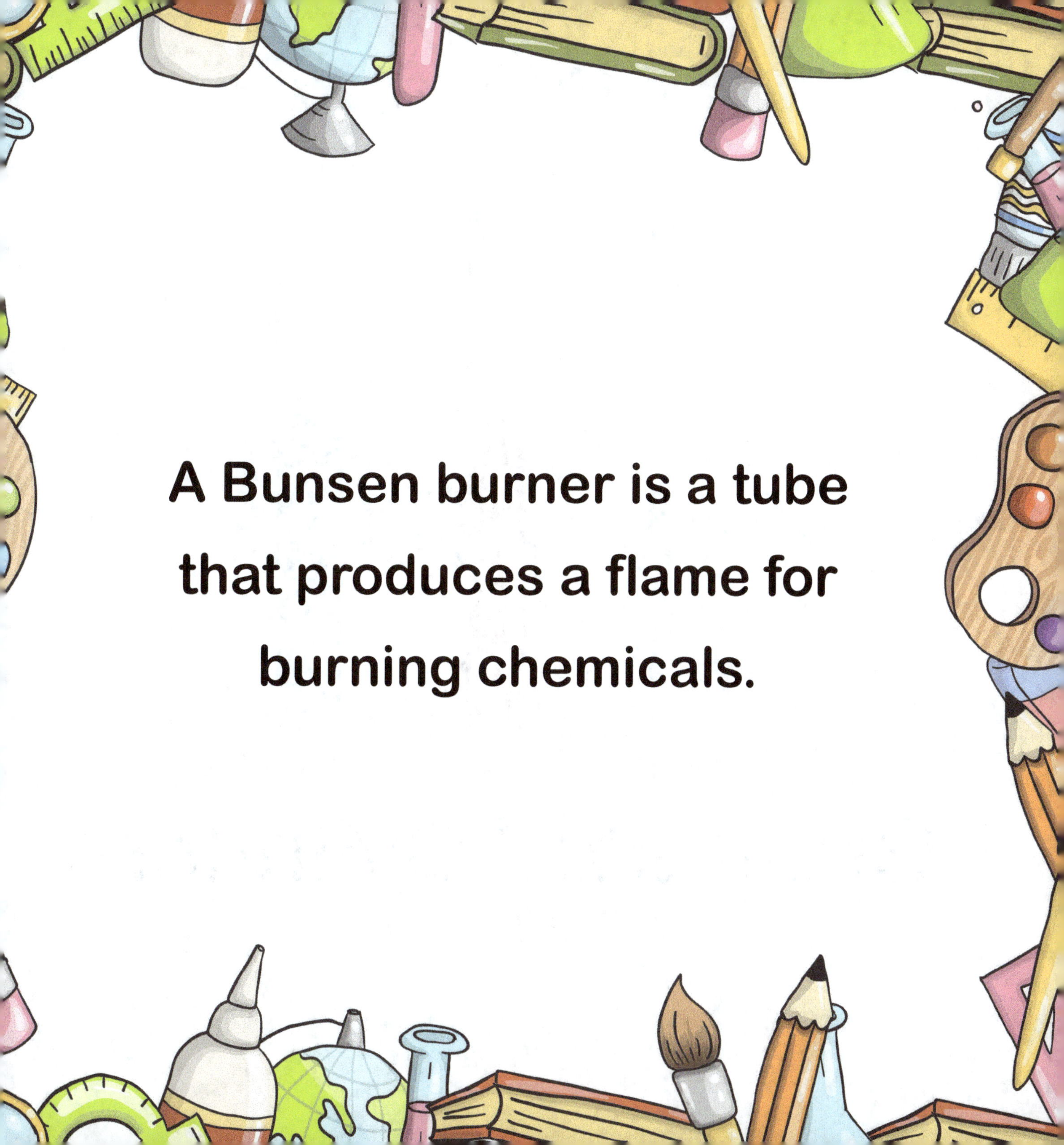

A Bunsen burner is a tube that produces a flame for burning chemicals.

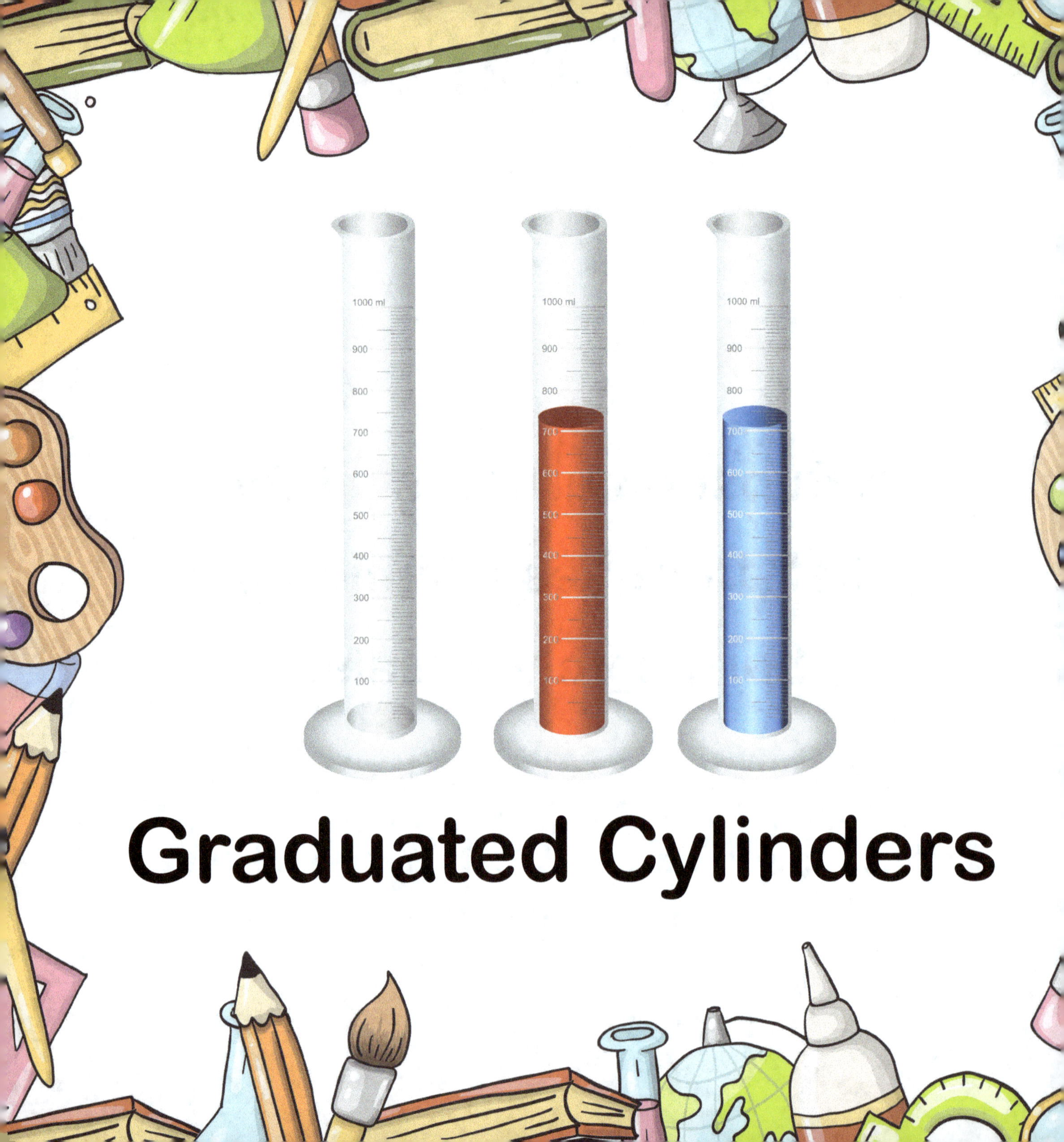

Graduated Cylinders

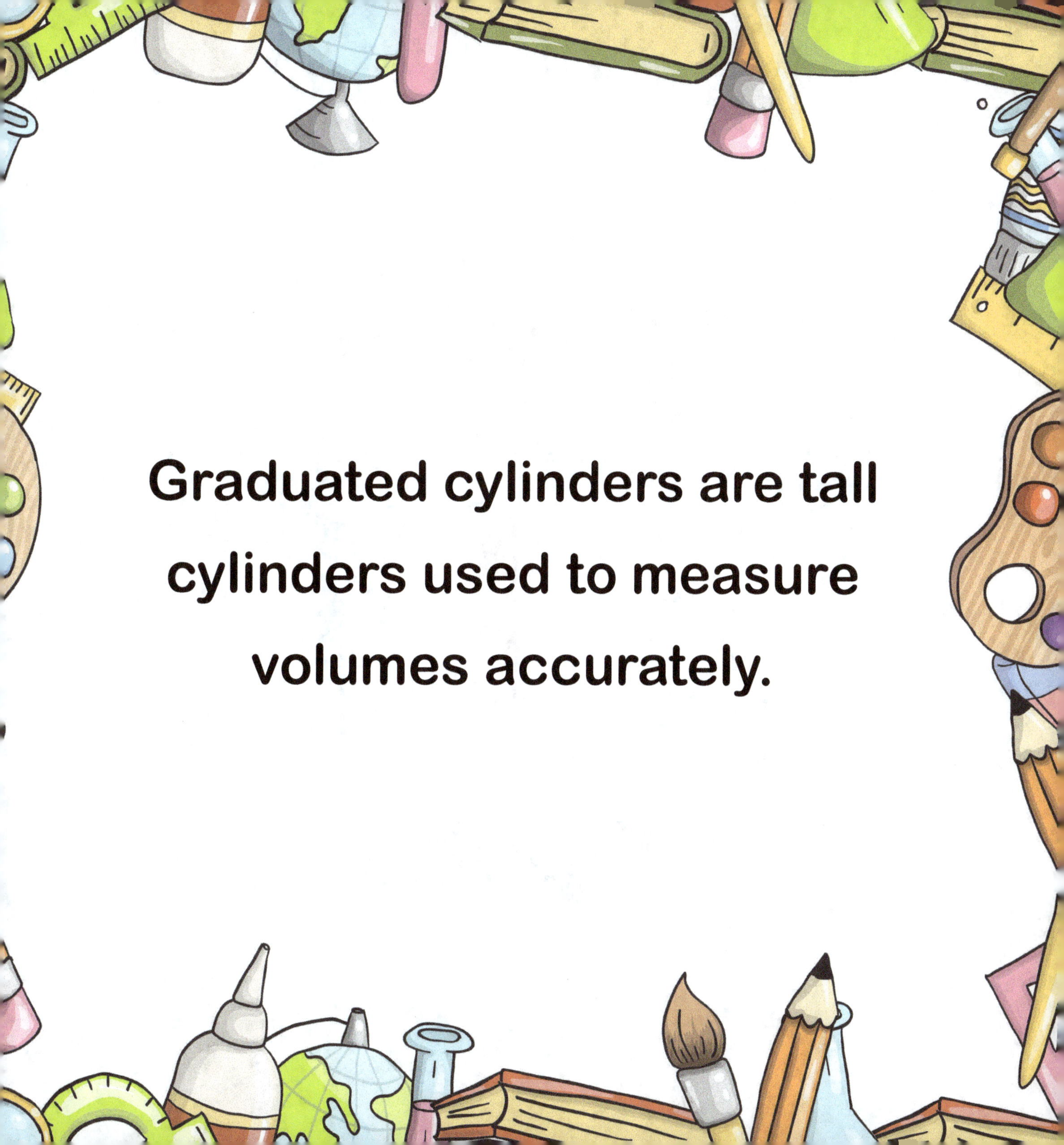

Graduated cylinders are tall cylinders used to measure volumes accurately.

Pipette

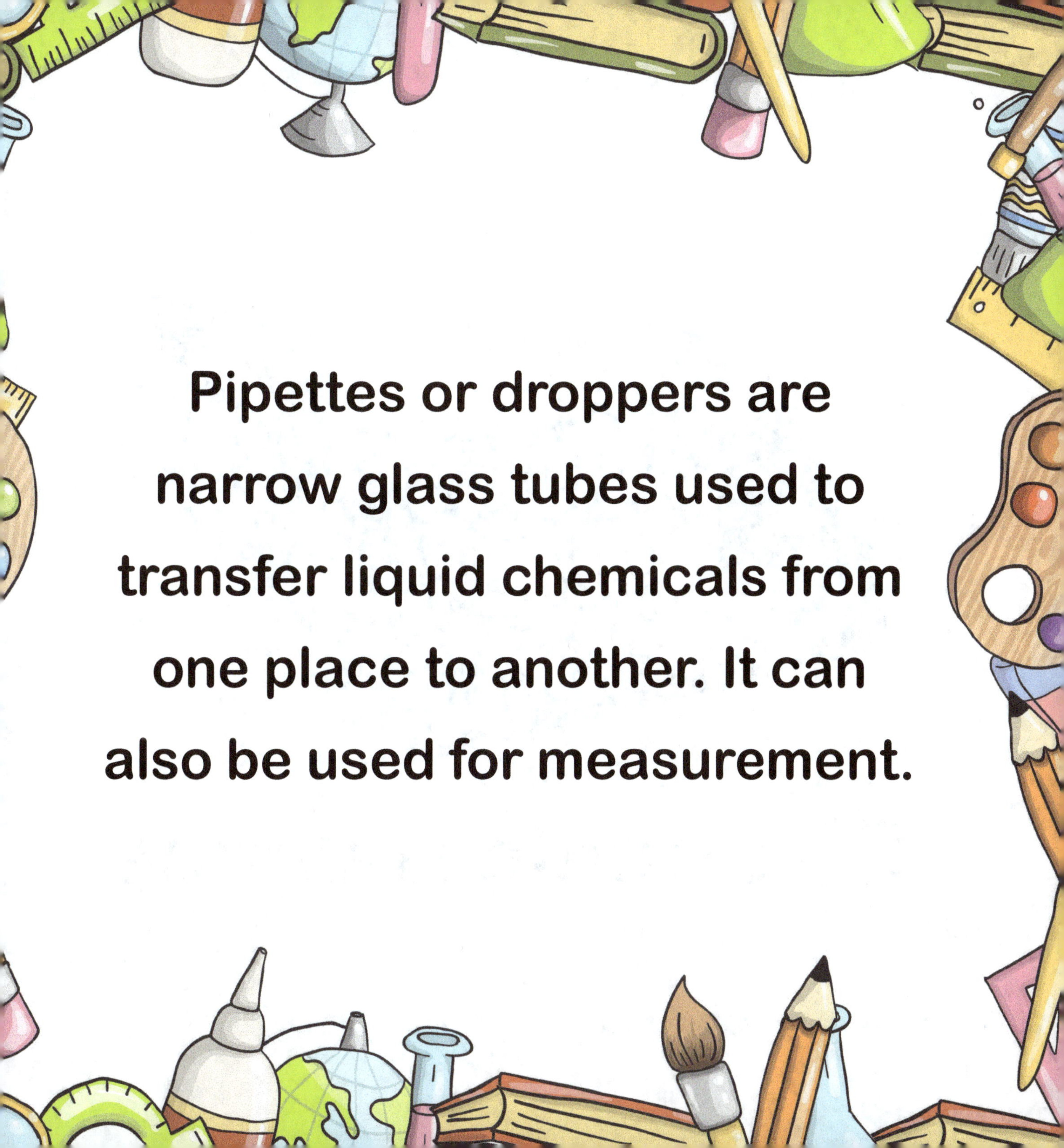

Pipettes or droppers are narrow glass tubes used to transfer liquid chemicals from one place to another. It can also be used for measurement.

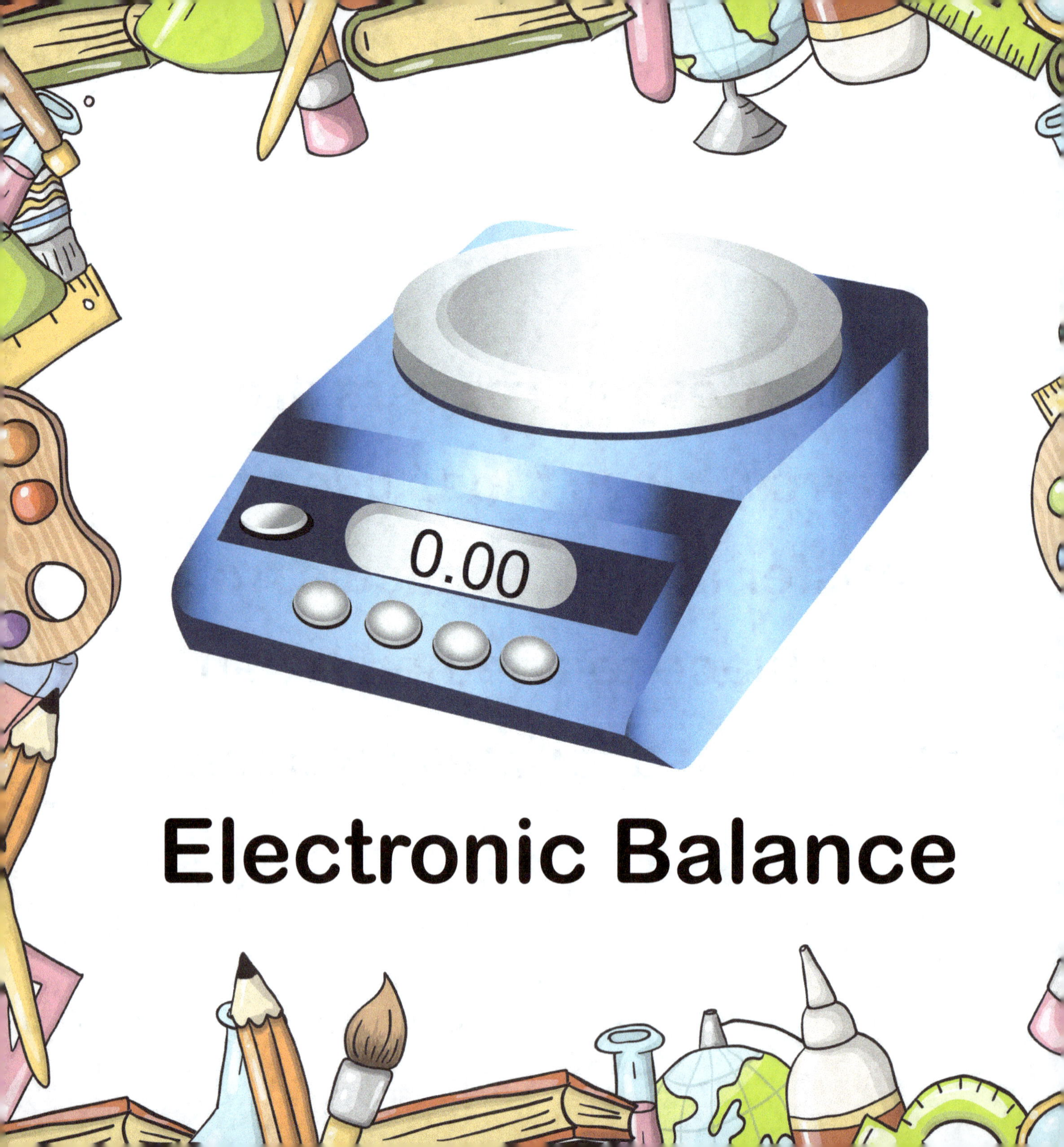

Electronic Balance

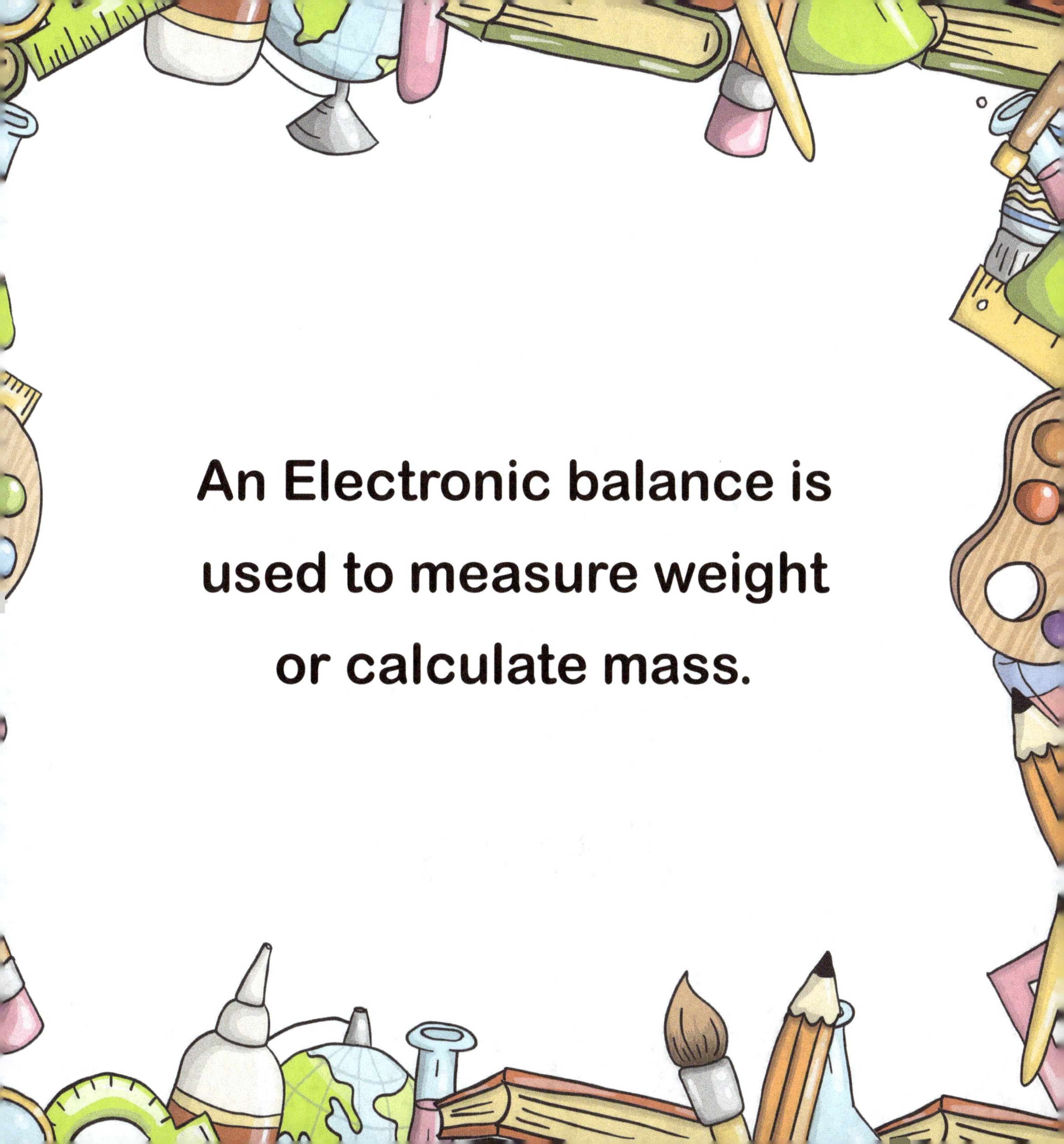

An Electronic balance is
used to measure weight
or calculate mass.

Funnels

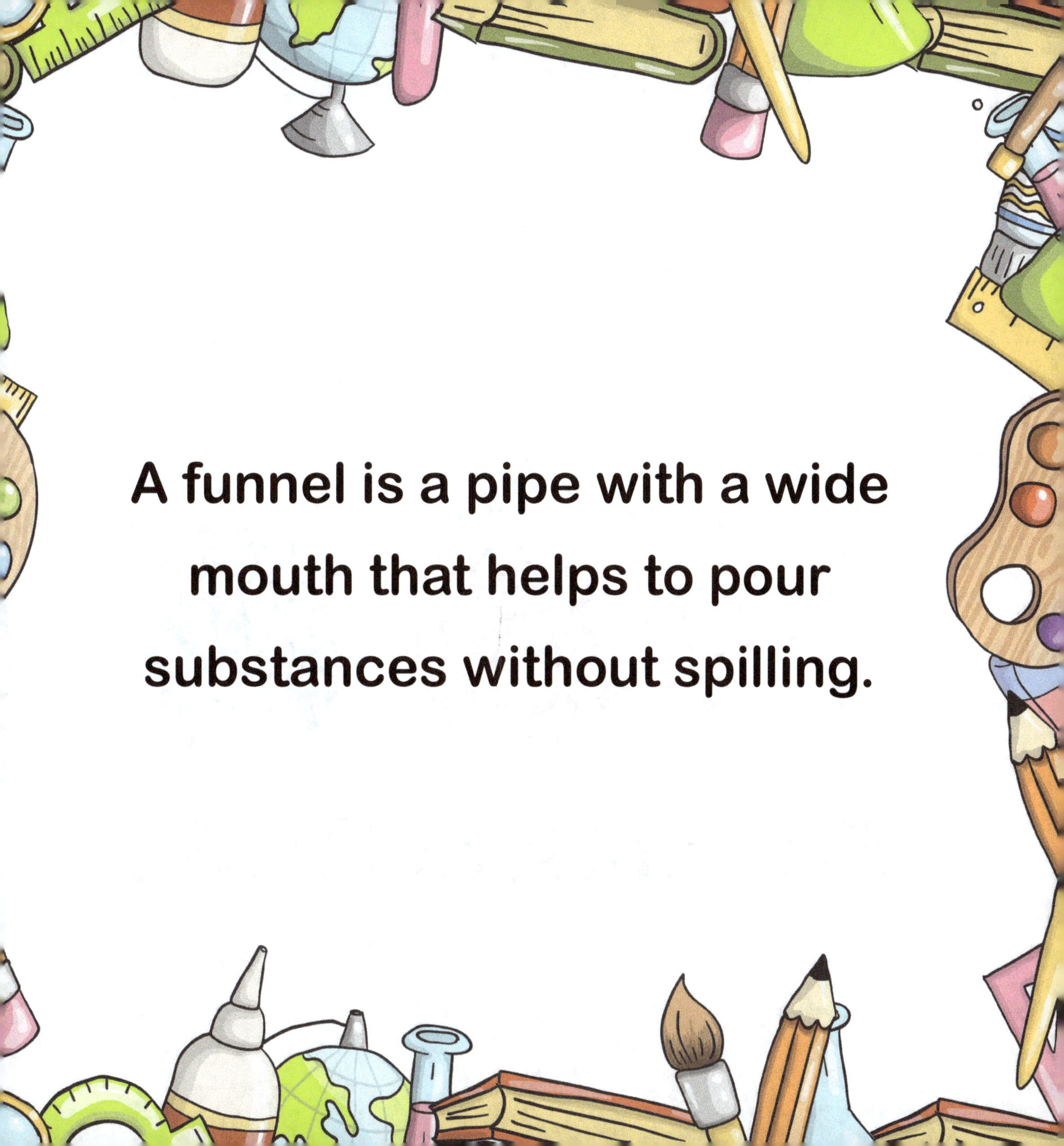

A funnel is a pipe with a wide mouth that helps to pour substances without spilling.

Flat-bottom Flasks

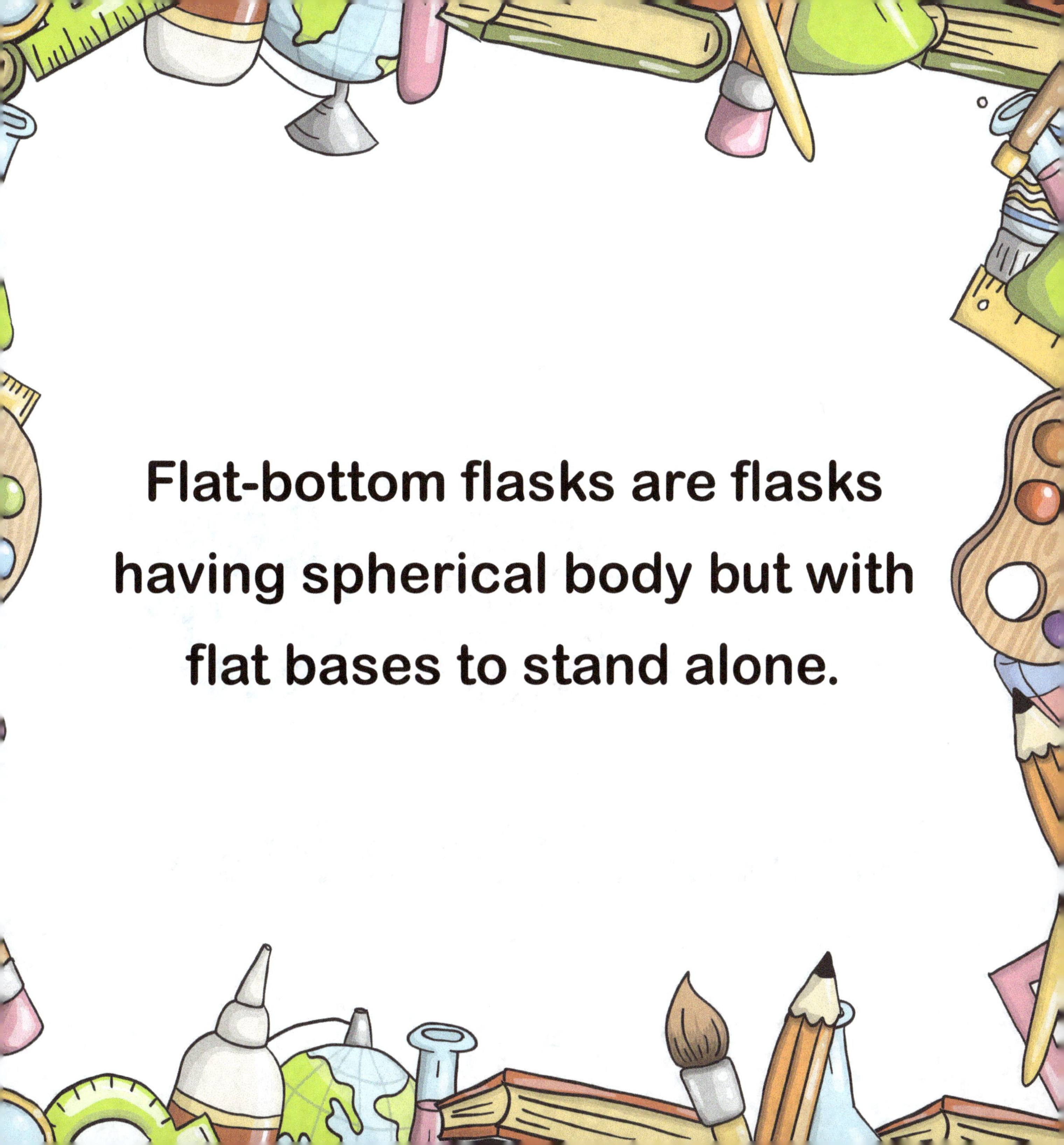

Flat-bottom flasks are flasks having spherical body but with flat bases to stand alone.

Round-bottom Flasks

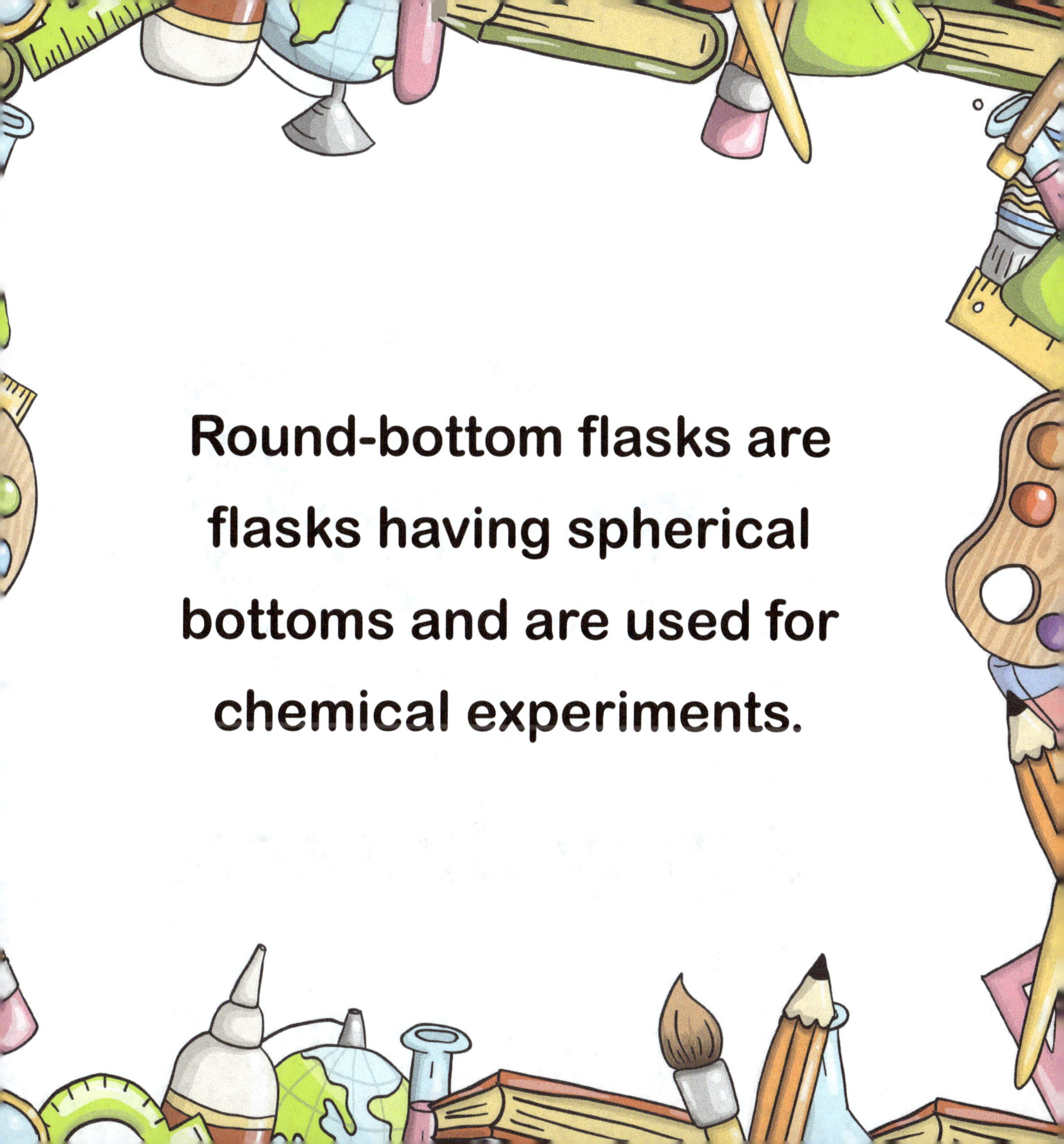

Round-bottom flasks are flasks having spherical bottoms and are used for chemical experiments.

Safety Glasses

Glasses are used to protect our eyes while doing experiments.

Mortar and Pestle

Mortar and pestle is used to grind solids into powder.

Scoopula

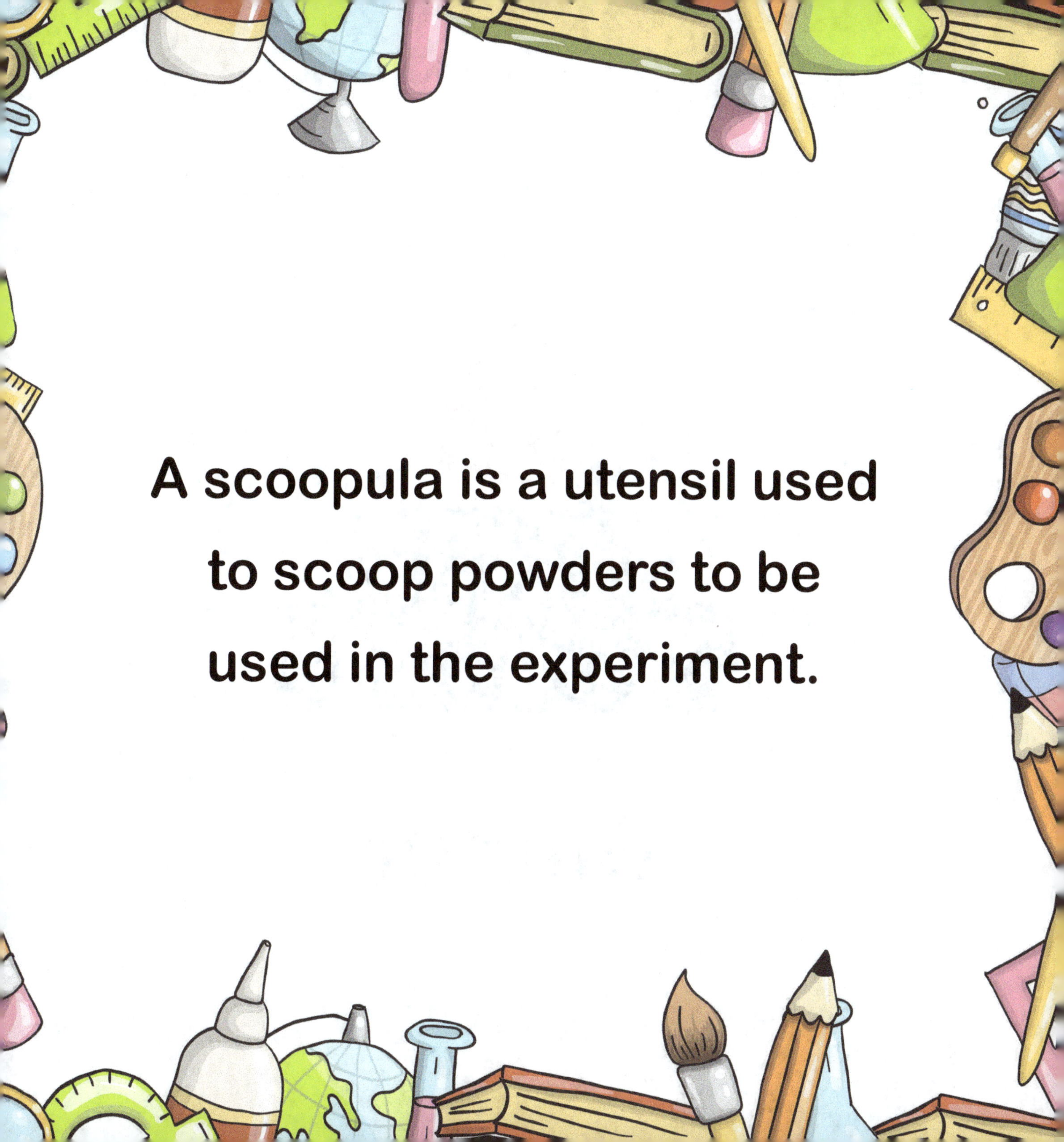

A scoopula is a utensil used
to scoop powders to be
used in the experiment.

Burner

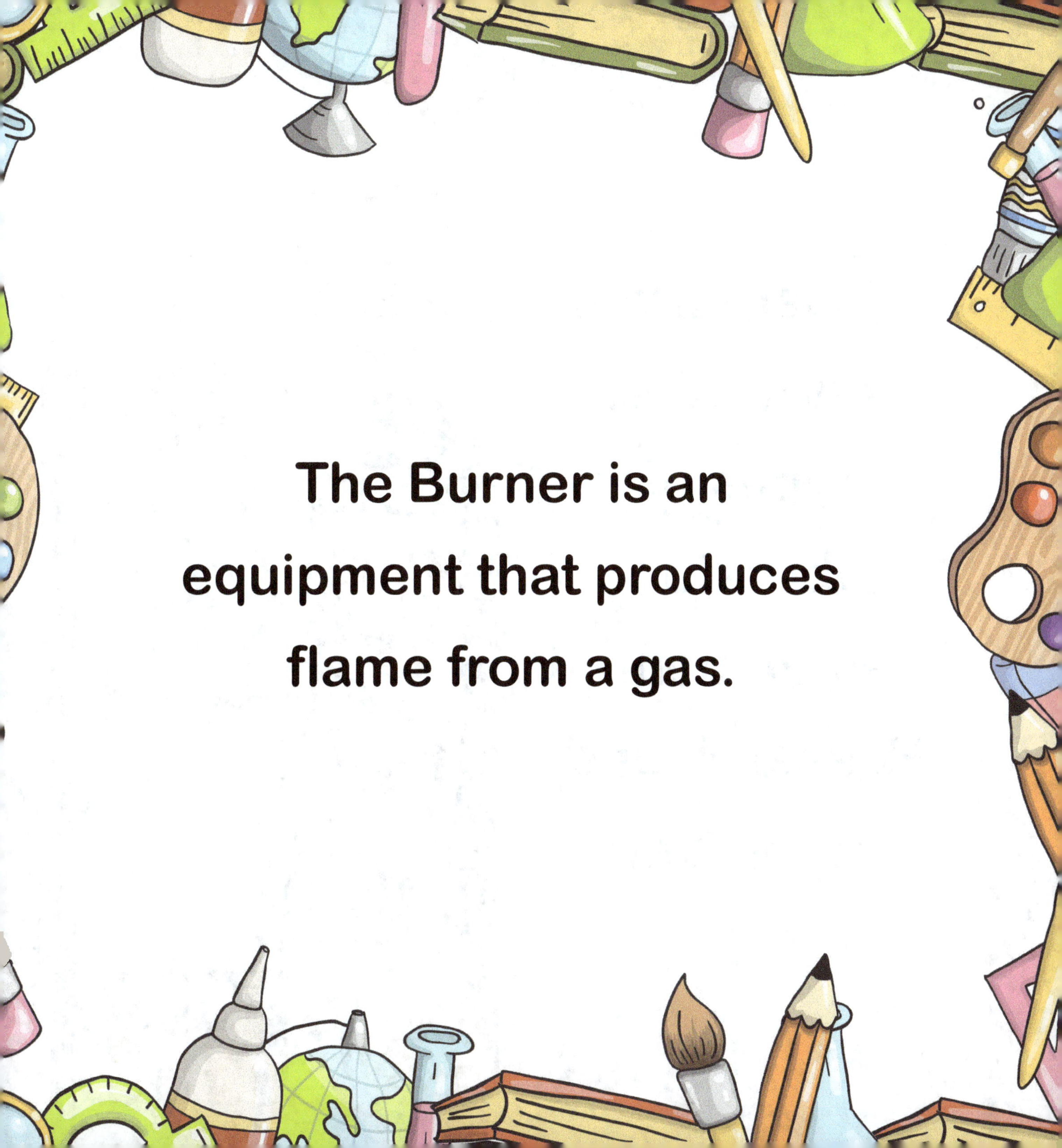

The Burner is an equipment that produces flame from a gas.

There are many other types of laboratory equipment. Research and have fun!

Visit
BABY PROFESSOR
EDUCATION KIDS
www.BabyProfessorBooks.com
to download Free Baby Professor eBooks
and view our catalog of new and exciting
Children's Books

www.ingramcontent.com/pod-product-compliance
Lightning Source LLC
Chambersburg PA
CBHW060619120726

48002CB00010B/3030